Little Spells

Jennifer K. Sweeney

New Issues Poetry & Prose

A Green Rose Book

New Issues Poetry & Prose
The College of Arts and Sciences
Western Michigan University
Kalamazoo, Michigan 49008

First Edition, 2015.

ISBN: 978-1-936970-33-9 (paperbound)

Library of Congress Cataloging-in-Publication Data:
Sweeney, Jennifer K.
Little Spells/Jennifer K. Sweeney
Library of Congress Control Number: 2014952966

Editor: William Olsen
Managing Editor: Kimberly Kolbe
Layout Editor: McKenzie Lynn Tozan
Assistant Editor: Alyssa Jewell
Art Direction: Nicholas Kuder
Design: Kai Asa Savon Wright
Production: Paul Sizer
                    The Design Center, Frostic School of Art
                    College of Fine Arts
                    Western Michigan University
Printing: McNaughton & Gunn, Inc.

Little Spells

Jennifer K. Sweeney

New Issues

WESTERN MICHIGAN UNIVERSITY

Also by Jennifer K. Sweeney

How to Live on Bread and Music
Salt Memory

For Liam Greenleaf

Contents

Five: *gloss and grain*

I think this is what God must look like, an egg.

—Margaret Atwood

field accomplice

Abandoning the Hives

From barn rafters, antique hives hang
queenless,
paperworks delicate as ash,
scaffold and cell mended thick with wax.

Wake up, the currents of bees have fled
this hour of seed
dark imaginings in their wake—
unsweet feverless drone.

Comb the hillside for sleepwalkers
drowsy on some chemical spool or
beg the swarm box to dance.
Everything depends on this refusal of happiness.

No one knows what they know.
A row of empty jars fills with sunlight.

Call and Response

There are mnemonics for remembering bird calls,
a goldfinch's airy *Po-ta-to chip!*
or the Inca dove's bleak *no-hope*. That spring,
a pair of meadowlarks pleaded *But-I-DO-love you*
from the maple boughs
and I thought how our bodies
exude their own churling mantras:
in the past, *I-am-no-good*
then, *please-just-breathe just-breathe.*
As morning throbbed light,
a new chant through Northern woods—
here-I-am where-are-you?—
the red-tailed vireo weaving a nest
of lichen, bark, web
while cowbirds prey on her eggs
leaving the mother to mourn the disappeared
work of her body in a solo
of call and response. Each month
our love offered up its question
to the world. *Here-I-am Where-are-you?*
as the ovums rose and disintegrated
silently. We walked along scrolls
of ocean, crows jagging the cliffs
like elaborate shadows and felt the specific
answer of *Not-yet Not-yet.*

Field Accomplice

She lives in a grove cottage, her mossy vapors
seep out the cracked stone door.

She flies around for hours begging me
to catch her in my throat.

Legally blind, she wears thick glasses
in which the future is inscribed in tintype.

Dwarf star with one eye on the moon.
A hired mourner I do not know how to fire.

She keeps a diary of pocket ghosts,
spends autumn putting dead leaves back on the trees.

When I look her up in the dictionary, it says:
rubicon   melting snow   emptied egg   ornate mercy
lo and behold   darkling   to beckon   to muddle

She prefers a collage of the sea instead of the sea.

Occasionally she offers practical advice:
forget renovation, a dark horse can do a lot
for a lackluster house.

Begging bowl I carry, tipped, hollow
like a desert bone murmuring prayers for rain.

No one can see them but there are women
who walk through bare fields carrying bread in their hands.

Lend to me this grain.

Little Spells

We are not witches as fable stoops us
hunchback over caldrons, not women
hobbled sinister by absence though we know
there are tides in our blood that lean us
toward some ancient clock. Still
if ox marrow soup is suggested, the pot readies
and if we return from the Chinese market
with a rough bag of earth tea, our house steeps
in the dank reduction of bark and root,
cold air cut heavy with mist.
We may have eaten goose eggs, raw
garlic and sweetbreads, charged our bathwater
with carnelian and held our noses as we threw
back shots of chlorophyll and kombucha.
We may have made closet altars,
placed bowls of royal pollen beneath our beds
and because someone swore it worked,
our underwear may have all gone orange, pockets
filled with quartz turtles, a moonstone at the throat.
If we turn out to be the end of the line,
there are other circles that will flare
like a small cosmos, we know that
creation is a field and a cave and we will be there
churning some broad-winged flurry from the ether.
We know we are not dying but we are
wading in a time-out-of-time
kept afloat by little spells. When will we again
be so studious with our will, omnipresent
of spark and silence and all the rough
honey it takes to set a life in motion?
We are not witches but we know
how to flick the last seeds
of air from a needle
and ease it into the womb
with reverie and we know magic
is its own making,
the power, if there be one,
not in the sung pot or expelled frog

but the fastidious busying
through the terrible
artistry of so fierce a care
as did my dear friend when her boy was born still,
secretly pumping milk through the spring
so that daily she poured a blue cup
over her garden until the blooms ached through.

Sleep Theory

In the long history of failed nights
I read field guides in the grocery store

parking lot. Along the empty
double-wide streets, the trick of the moon

reflected in apartment windows
like a row of monocles raised in a theater,

some silvery beacon fished from the cosmos
to help us outlast the dark.

Sound of water being poured
when there is no glass.

Bouquet of shadows in the empty bowl.
In the long history of stalled dreams, the one

about the sisters who wore
milkweed dresses. I was invisible

yet helped them escape through
the forest because I knew

they would survive.
Though I may have thought it so, night

is not a bread-trail leading into
or out of a forest.

I read a handbook for the modern shepherd,
outdated maps salvaged

from a grade school dumpster.
The hours slip in

and out of matter, head
a tumble of fretwork.

Inkling, I follow the rusted gate.
Rustle the cherry tree. Leave me hungry.

On Not Being an Axeman

Swing the apple blade,
maul the ash. A cutting
of late honeysuckle
in a penny vase. I have romanced
hawks and fieldstone
and the notion that in another life
I would have made a fine axeman,
splitting knots in the flannel dusk
to make clean a work of private
knowledge. Is a life more than
a landscape of choices so minor
they are shrugs of mind
that impose a narrative
grander at a distance?
To breathe sharply this dark
air, ignore the animal
dash and rustle and fix steady
on the turning of, returning to
the task of my whatever
hour. Like the tree
etched with secrecy,
striations wound in a brindly mass,
grooveworks and spirals
grow crooked the unsplittable.
How much I fail at knowing
trees and my neverlasting self
is what binds us.
It might have been such a shrug
not becoming axeman,
or *man, fly, tree.* Can I know then
it is not a violence
this splitting of the wood,
(can I feel) the arc
cutting no-sound into sound
stump-stopped and waving through
my unstruck body?

Happy People

They do have one blue secret.
It's about gravity.
They don't much care
the way it can clod a life
with freight.
And their eyes—
why not here
poised across a rib?
No wet marbles.
No inquisition.
Just saying the word *turquoise*
is to swim it.
See how easily they lean in,
come toward?
The liquid body buoyed along
that sail of air.

White October

You cannot let go the ember,
cinnamon and rust,
everything husked and shaking

paper skins, the hay-sweet
evening, auburn and cold
rooted from a seasonal childhood.

You search it in the October skyline
but the day is only white
over skirted mountains.

You could lose yourself
crawling the car around coast cliffs
and all the ways you've wished

for disappearance
lower down in veils,
take a fragment of memory or

desire back into the perpetual
dusk of ocean,
wrinkling and unwrinkling

its surf and glide.
You're searching for a little
fire, anything aglow

on the mauve-brown bluffs,
but that's not the point
this blurred world is making,

white October with its white pumpkins
and pearly pampas grass.
Thin as a plume

it's something about surrender,
how your need is a shade less
in this fieldrush of cloud.

The person you love is beside you
and the rest of your life is a big question—
it's something about the cornsilk

of one two three hawks
swooping low
into the numinous.

Blessing of Hours, Curse of the Horse

In the middle of the field,
may your horse float
against the furze, fog of morning
like unfinished sleep, may the wet
cockle of his eye be the only clarity,
your skin blurry as on some shore
may fall a lone shadow
that points to no tree.
May the hills, luminous and green,
make green your intention
as silent as wishes
for daughters issued at birth.
May you fall in a nettle patch
May you wade in the brine
May updrafts wail clean off black
waves, a red stone in your throat
for longing
a no-stone for memory.
In the middle of the year
may your horse's gait in the uncut
grasses be so deeply swaying
your bones shine in their paper bindings
and if he must eat, may you offer
your hand, your hand in his
dry mouth, the scars and the conscience
of pleasure out of this world join.

cliffside narrative

Anthology of Fairytales, with Instructions and a Coda

If you have enough love, you can transform a pumpkin, a crab,
blood clot into daughter

If you seek a magic remedy, give birth to snakes,
snails, pots, apples, twigs,
a monster-child who will consume

If you bargain with the devil, you will become the devil
unless you are already the devil

If it is broken and you are willing,
If you stop want, want harder, if you will it, chant it,
if you ascend the hall of mirrors and can identify
the motherself, then, then,
the inscrutable word that hangs you

Gingerbread Man

in the shape of a boy there was / in the edge of a wood everyone
little and old the house empty in the hunger for him / life was
happy-but-for, sour bread that tasted of forest / there was a hunger
then an idea then a shape then a hunger / and wasn't it grand when
oven he leapt / wasn't it a terror to want him

Hans-my-Hedgehog

i wouldn't care if he were dispassionate as an axe
idiot as an iamb i wouldn't care
idle as a box of echoes
foul as a swampbed he were
wayward awkward coward backward
tough as a heel of bread
i wouldn't care if he were feverless as a paper moon
a whiplock sealed in ice o care i would
mute as poison's quiet knowledge
what would i care if he were if only he were
loused stumbling felled
borderless as sedge rising from sedge

Snow White

water in the lake run dry my dear water in the lake run dry

      there is no greater white these days all glass

and the mice do our mending when we wake

      poison in the glass we were happy dear

wiping the curses from your mouth

      snow blight and the pain of kings made near

and the lies do our rending as we wait

Tatterhood

hostage in the conditional the beggar holds the queen in her hands / a rose and a weed, coin of chance grinding their futures to the dissolve of have: have-not / to cut a wish in half / serve it with one hand / tatter says only do, tatter wants to live too / dear bruising flowers / devour them both the queen in her mouth / daughters, bear the twin seeds of good and evil

Thumbelina

who will plant a barley seed
who will plant a fish
who will sing a water well
who will raise the ditch
who will drift in poppy time
who will eye the spark
what thread will stitch the voice that leaves
thumbprints in the dark
what dark erases the mother
when a daughter springs from wish
what sentence does she fold into
what barely budded hiss

Iroko Tree

Our village-without-child,
face the Iroko go mad and die
still we knelt daily
a spirit fearsome and good

some people promise goats, some people promise rams

I offered you when you were only a word
backward sea of my body
I would have said
anything

some people promise hair, some people promise bone

daughter red as palm oil
it claimed your voice sinking into earth
turned me to bird, no mother was I
red as palm oil: daughter, keep singing

Rapunzel

beware witches with opulent gardens / be fair wife of increased
longing / come back to the hunger that undoes / come back to
pleasure always the woman / in once-upon towers braiding the
consequences / be unborn / eat / grow your own rope

Sleeping Beauty

to all the waters we went it cannot be expressed and the vows so
sorry we were / all the waters to no purpose the pilgrimages to no
end and the days so sorry were / and tired in our seeking when she
came from the ether it was no simple *however* / it was gold-back
and bellsound rung toward future all the waters it wept / unknowing
at the wheel a good woman and alone handed the needle kindly and
oh quiet blood it cannot be expressed our waiting became her
waiting / redsky, redbird forgive us a life we grow tired in our sleep

*   *   *

The insistence of *not-yet* even in the bread that took hours to chew. *Hold on* the voice kept, *everwhile*. On with the ordinary grace of washing hands when dirty, shutting lights in the empty room. Meanwhile the trifold of winter expands to a groundswell. Meanwhile the slipstream. Then the moon is breaking up with you all over again and you knew it was coming but awful just the same. When the rehearsal consumes, unravel the narrative. In the vaulted forest, hear owls, bullfrogs speak from their whole bodies. Downturned bowl of bird-matter ovoid in your hands. *Oh void,* says the heart, *is no negation, to know each curve of the empty, a singular attention that draws you starkly to threshold.* Place the nest on the windowsill where it houses a tryst of light. Dear nobodies, this unfit earth.

blue hush in the blood meridian

Beyond a Longing Lying Bluely

Or that I am missing it entirely.
What of the energy folded inside the rye,
enough wind to lift the field, fire

to silk the mountain.
That we might be stoking something other
than time with our bright silences

earth's wood song braided
not from what is given but what is withheld.
Today I took out my questions again

and polished them to a shine,
student of listening for a quiver
of blood, have I been hearing it wrong?

Beyond the fact of a longing in pieces
lying bluely, see how easily
the world conspires to make more

of itself with its not-much spark and sap.
How a dove lifts a small vault of air
across the grass and I am part of it.

Janice Pockett

Her name like a warning at the edge of the woods
and also   *green metallic bicycle   empty envelope*
butterfly-under-rock.
Whoever made her disappear did it entirely.
Had the kennel released its hounds
the dogs would have found nothing
before the decades of nothing.
How far back to trace a vanishing—
butterfly that crossed her path days before just so,
the one her hands finally caught
and the impulse that made her hide
it under *that rock*. Afternoons later
how she wanted to retrieve it or
the time it took to scavenge the drawers
for an envelope to carry it home and so
and so. No. That isn't right.
No life should lean on such fine margins.
Janice Pockett, we 70s children sleeved your name
in our bodies like an orange flash in the wind.
Your name became prayer.
Your mother is still searching the woods
for the rock, the room for the envelope,
the quick bright wings for your voice.
When we rode off on banana seats toward
our granted days, we wanted to bring you home.
When we said your name, we whispered.

The Dance Student

We wound our bodies up at nine a.m.
alternating blue and green leotards
for the days of the week.
I stood on the end facing the corner-mirror
so when the accompanist played the sonorous plié
from behind the helm of the piano
and our arms carved the cold air in unison,
it looked like one woman twelve layers deep.
The snow fell heavy and slow
as our legs extended, hollow of ankle
nesting on barre, torquing our hips
into a new architecture.
Against the landscape of mirror,
our audience was reflection, all stance and blur,
eyes huge against the pull of bunned hair.
Who knows the moment
when we are most real to ourselves?
At five, staring at myself
in a pantyhose display at the Kmart,
stacked wall of mirrored L'Eggs,
my hundred concave faces gazing back.
Or during the silent snip of haircuts
arms folded beneath cape
until handed the small mirror and circled
around to approve the back of my head.
Sometimes we ended class flat on our backs,
all spun-out, braids of muscle clenched
along the spine. What a relief
to be past the adagio,
petit allegro, sweep of grand jeté,
past falling off-balance, the wash of pain
held in our line of watchful faces.
I still feel that papery dancer fighting
against her bones, that oblong
child repeated in a row of eggs
like they will perpetually peer
out for a sign of recognition,
some rough nod of approval
from the surface of things.

The Returning

I had forgotten the gravitas of true autumn,
how the days become lessons in light,
cross-hatched frescoes subsumed

by the steely wash of regret.
Someone was up late moving our rocks again,
midnight at the stone wall.

Windows atilt, buckling doors,
the houses have grown so old.
Condemned porches hinging in the wind

echo the season's language of return:
to turn over, go back.
Part the spiderwebbed air,

part the slipshod
heave ho of leaf-rot.
Every few days a boy asks to rake our lawn.

I decline three times.
What touches me most about people is their effort.
Sonar of a power saw,

sound of a roof being mended.
They held a pumpkin regatta
on Lake Michigan,

hollowed out the elephantine gourds
and raced them downstream.
There's nothing grave about that.

Turn around, turn in,
turn pumpkinward to the horizon.
But then the salvaged light

of fence posts far older than men
and all equations lead back to longing.
The boy knocks again, wants to borrow my rake,

for a neighbor's house he says.
From the window I watch him sweep two strokes,
give a cagey look then hop his bike

and even though he is slow enough for me
to run after, I don't.
I want to see

the teetering gait of his getaway,
rake raised like a mast
sailing out into the gray night.

The Stone Fitter

Most dreams reflect a day's thinking
like the one where all the windows
were shattered but otherwise intact
the morning after we shut the storms
and the new cold howled
at the glass. The same people
pass like hours the day wears.
Gray woman with gray dog
hunched in misgiving
plods slowly through the snow.
River-man collecting cans in a stroller,
part moss, part leather,
rounds the block at three.
A life on pause.
A life boxed for a future opening.
When I grow shadowy, a hammer
pounds the distance, steady downbeat
of work, and a girl walks in step.
Each time her foot hits the pavement,
the hammer sounds or the hammer makes her
walk or her walking makes it pound.
I keep three rows of six apples in the fruit tray.
There is pleasure in tending the vacancy.
Keep rose quartz in my pocket and wait
for it to bloom.
I dream of a stone wall, a zen
of gray-white smooth as monks' bowls,
rows fit together by an intention so serious
there is comfort in knowing someone
thought to make this, Protean work
of listening for what next comes,
even if the maker is not present
and only reveals her art
beneath the lapidary surface of my sleep.

Salmon and Blood Orange

When the paycheck's delayed
and the kitchen is draped
in shadow, we reach back
into the cupboard dark to sustain.
Sea kelp we couldn't rehydrate,
burdock root gnarled to boar knuckle.
From the macabre still life
of the fruit bowl, we revive
our remains into something
unrepeatable and the haphazard cuisine
stitches the work of our days.
Sometimes a tapas of bold flavor
or just muddled in obscurity
like the night we finally opened
the anchovies and laid them
on an improvised crust.
This is what it means to be a family.
We sit down with our bounty
of endings, last wedge
of salmon and blood orange—

Winter, Parenthetical

Most of the houses had tilted floors

and mineral sinks and felt more like finding ourselves at sea
than midwest, the legless tables and torched couches, all promised
to be removed if we signed a contract. When we found one
with two bats in the bedroom and a dismantled piano
on the front porch, we agreed.

I had wished to live in a country of bad weather and nested
inside a winter inside a winter inside a long night.
I saw with my left eye. I slept with my right.

Of all the things I was I was mostly cold

and though *cold* and *sad* had different origins they were twin ghosts.
I longed for a root cellar and filled bags of apples and squash.
There was the feeling we had fallen upon hard times which made us
feel nostalgic and prophetic though we were neither of these things.
A sky of leaves lowered and the bare trees filled with nests.
Spiders slept like ink spots in gauzy webs under the staircase.
The bats scratched between the walls for weeks. We abided
with the knowing, then the silence.

Drunken circles of footprints in the snow. Footprints leading
to the bathroom window in the sober eye of another Sunday.
We had to make calls to ask strangers to remove the obstacles.

I tried to explain the problem of inheritance in an office
lined with impossible babies, blue hush in the blood meridian,
how many others shadowed in the lineage.

Be data clocked to a prime. Be clay. Locust.

3 am and a shoeless man clawing at our front, our back door.
Off his meds we held him there speaking through the glass.
This is as difficult as it is to talk to anyone, I thought,
watching his sock-feet zigzag the snow to the flashing car.

Ida bushels grew cidery in the damp dark next to the stash of needles
that came with the freezer-packed vials of Follistim.
Derived from the urine of menopausal nuns. I fingered the gold cross
sunk to the bottom of the jewelry box.

The next blizzard someone leashed a black dog to our porch.
We cooked what we had in soup pots and did not leave
and did not know. How silent all that time, its body
half-froze on the fourth day, but alive.

I want to go back. To before I knew this would be so hard.
To the beginning of us when I first dreamt our child
was a wood sprite we chased through redwood trees.

The temperature held at a single degree.
Two cardinals flying out of a nun's black habit.
Seven eyes on the Japanese sweet potato.

Of all the things I was I was not. Not-surfacing. Not-agreeing.
Not-finished. Knot-breathing.

Listen for the groundswell beneath the vacancy. Listen
for the vacancy brilliant in its question. The work of the river
flux-froze and arching backward the way a woman makes a life
of trying to listen inside her body.

For headaches, feverfew. For cold womb, false unicorn root.
To ward off hibernating insects, osage oranges in the windowsills.
For twin ghosts, divide fire in two equal parts.

I found a barefoot doctor from the Chinese countryside
displaced in upper Michigan. She fixed a track of needles
along my spine and told me to lie down. I felt the suggestion
of a bed of nails but otherwise no sensation at all.

We had to ask strangers to remove the obstacles.

Snow fell on the ultrasound. We searched the static for eggs.
The needle injected its promise and again, a courage of waiting.
For days the harvest attempted division. *Only one* the nurse said
quietly over the phone, *nothing to freeze.*

The icicles were two stories long and became a kind of fortress.
During brief sun, a shipwreck of ice plowed the house on all sides,
then formed a moat. The iris bulbs I planted in autumn foolishly
sprouted, brief nudge of purple bombarded by a second winter
and life too sparked briefly in me then snuffed out and there was
no sensation at all.

What to place in this raw absence, this

pre-life or, *o grief*, non-life, your reverse elegy orbiting around me.
Some butterflies have a seven year molt. No spent decade
in the spun loom. How to mend these quiet rooms,
beg it raw-kneed, crawl the walls and take to the woods.
Let the flock breathe the questions. If the body be old,
cold moon—then polish, do. Finish, done.

Blindness Training Center

They're in the talking crosswalk again
with blackout masks and guide sticks
scouring double lanes
while I wait in the shell of my car.

The light bleats red and they follow
the vowels of a teacher who calls, curbside.
I can see the O of her mouth but do not hear
her voice, a slow fog blurring the periphery.

New groups arrive weekly before winter
makes a Siberia of Michigan,
students of the waning year.
I pass them on trips to the grocery store,

the preserve where I hike a ragged loop.
Frogs have begun sleeping
in the understory of Asylum Lake,
where they will hang weightless

like a colony of stars until spring,
the surface lidded thick with ice,
knowing or not, time
continues in slow circles above.

I carry my melancholy home with the milk
and bread. A stand of maples,
knife against grain in the cold
kitchen. How to *not-see*,

learn through balance,
nudge, everything noise
and space—is it a small betrayal
tying fold behind head

so they might be ready when shadow

is greater than moss? What is
ready, what new attention
gathers in to listen for the color

of textures underfoot and how can it be
measured, what is lost, to realize
life requires also such quiet
and uncelebrated restraint.

Doc Solves Mystery of Frida Kahlo's Infertility

—*MSNBC headline, 2012*

Old story, doctor—to bravo your name
into history, swoop in horse-mounted
and save her by brandishing what she knew:
We owe it to Frida! Until now, no one has ever
connected her infertility to the street car accident.
She gave the inside of her body, her open
veins, twisted spine, nails piercing her cheeks.
My womanhood raped by a metal bar, she said,
the bar forcing through her pelvis.
You do not need to wax on about *The Broken Column*
or sit her down sixty years later in your patient seat
with the damaged flower of your diagnosis
blooming around you. She left nothing
to complete. Your first desire to save,
that boyish charm, never involved asking.
Have you made a life from this silence?
Go back to the asylum light.
As if you are suddenly *fish*, that otherly new,
change everything you presume about being a woman.

Tendril-minded

The train sounds more often
since the latest shadow jumped the tracks.
On warm days I get out for a walk,

cross a few scratchings off a list.
This wasn't how it was supposed to be
makes a bad mantra.

But all the same.
It is the everyday that haunts.
A gradual greening,

assemblage of fungus
skirting rain-clogged trunks.
The train drags its warning diagonally

through town over and over.
I peer into the woods with no need to hurry home.
See a deer in the brush, then another

until every blond branch seems to be deer
and the herd of them gallops through
a perfectly empty river.

Across Useless Bay

Blue-gray body in gray shallows in gray
fog light, you emerge a lithe calligraphy,
at once liquid and statue.
A flapping of ducks circle,
the otter undulates past,
cattails plash in the salt wind—
does nothing ruffle?
When you step finally forth on stilt legs,
it is solemn as a monk's procession,
right then left in even time.
So you know time then—
contemplating the longing of your throat.
What silky notion are you searching
beneath the surface,
a design of shadow and glint
after so much nothing?
Rare lash of your neck,
beak like a scimitar cutting the water
for a swallow of sleek fish.
To be so present, taste
any bite like that.
But that's a glory I shackle to you, heron,
who are anonymous,
would attend the water all evening if it be
without the weight of patience,
hovering over glass,
as the last remnants of light let go.

Study of Family with Buckets

Their five figures take the shore
          with a purpose specific
                    as the beachgrass knit

across the eroded dune.
          The older boy bears a net
                    to drag the tide

of cockleshells and conch,
          luminosities and ruin
                    that exist only now

in the first naming.
          Sea cucumber. Mermaid's purse.
                    Minnows flecking their ankles,

the family bends toward surface
          regarding each fragment
                    as a whole.

Buckets fill with wrack and root
          glint of filament
                    scanned in singularity.

The mother spots a marbled patina
          and they sieve it up to the air—
                    two rockcrabs seamed in a compact link.

The mating is considered shyly, without shame,
          a study of armament and flesh—
                    this, the one thing responsible

for their presence.
          They attend to the world as equals,
                    for none of them have ever stood

in this water before
          with such circles
                    gathering at their feet.

Vespertine

Blue moon glows from the hollow
of the walnut tree where the rabid
raccoon homed in mid-July then
disappeared. Bless
the comings-and-goings that keep us
wanting. Geese pulse in, spread apart
as the flock breathes.
How to hold such leavings
or measure the way updrafts
of wind scatter the marsh
where red-winged blackbirds nest over water
because they have to and I am wrong
to say *beauty*, say *stay*—
it is I feel the bird's effort
as my own. When I walk at dusk
in the descending cold my feet
slap the sidewalk in even time.
They are trying to steady this world
that changes so fast because
I don't know how much I am capable of.
A tree becomes sawdust, lilac turns to hibiscus
to chrysanthemum, pumpkin faces soften
and cave and I nurse this fierce
wanting-to-go-back
to the first cell and begin again.

The Blueberry Pickers

—South Haven, MI

A season in time-lapse whisks by
wrinkled and wrong
where streets veer into distance
through unmapped towns
and the dusty community church
stands like a sentinel next to the freight tracks,
searchlight of the diner
blinking its worn constellation.
What is it to never leave a place—
tractor rusting in the wheat—
or to arrive here from Mexico,
a migrant family stashed in storage shacks
to wait out the rise of prized fruit,
the coveted hands of children
nimble enough to pluck blueberries
in noon heat without collapsing ripe skins.
When fingerprints are rinsed
away in the colander, jam preserved,
pies baked and ribboned in town fairs,
the workers emerge from hiding
in the dying light of August,
blue hands in pockets,
and make their silent exodus
from the back of beyond.

Year of the Ox

begins with cellar apples gone blue   tanglewood woven to bone
in the zero woods   solo bellow keen   pack on boxes   untidy
moon-cargo   woman mending, bird light   stack the papers
set the clock   drag the needle through the eye of night
the lesson is again   the lesson is wisteria   a mute swan returning
to roost   or there is no lesson   only footnotes to a prologue
align with a tide chart   keep count but start over after one hundred
begins with a tornado siren   begins with a coda   carry the rat
on your back, highlander   don't talk too much   a farewell letter
a stalk of boneset   gives way to tiny howlings

Aubade for the Thirteenth Hour

1

I reach into the sea
for your small hand
like a phantom limb—
that you will come when the bees

stop dying in the river,
when the moon has cycled 49 times
and the fish have surfaced the black
pond, momentary gasp when I decide

I no longer need you, swaddled
in folktales about women who create
a child out of mandrake root, gourd, snow
the effigy haunted blue in its silence.

Couldn't you feel my clutch
at street crossings? Didn't you want to
watch the world go by from the helm
of our laps?

2

We were told *give it a season you're both healthy* but when the fourth season came and went near the end of the year, how I was already addressing you, hovering on possibility, who may never rise into the magnitude of a pronoun. And who was dropping such things from the sky, small white egg intact but for a pinhole, nest upon nest under rotting leaves, and what creature wouldn't scavenge the forest for bloodlight, wouldn't meditate on the endless knot, so much like the inside of the female body? We released five koi into our pond, wrote a letter and left it beside a Buddha in the mountains. The grace that carried us into the thirteenth season was not elegant or laced with surrender, as the doctors recommended, but the kind a barred owl uses to fly into the head of any person walking near her nest during mating season.

3

Or I might wander cobbled alleys
follow a gas-lit hallway or half-door
where you will dangle your legs from a heavy chair
apple head centered under a clock
that ticks thirteen times after I arrive
and you will nod, more like the mother then
as if you knew I was coming
and had not been worried.

A ring of redwoods, bundle of leaves, the story
always the same though in this approximation
of you, something arrived. I won't say
it was enough, but long I searched you
a mythic child became rooted
to my psyche, provided an odd comfort
like the presence of a beloved

who has died. Maybe this *you*,
shadowy other, I made
out of thought to find a widening
place to enter back into the world.
If being is love, then *not-being*,
a wholly other kind of love.

$$\frac{58}{59}$$

still life with egg

Still Life with Egg

1

is unto itself   is architecture
woven of feather and bone
pebbled   cupped
painted without brush

is ceramic   lined with oyster skin
viscous   chalaza
tiny balloon for breathing
is vellum and sack

cradle   concentration
not tender nor hollow   is thaw
canvas   maraca   passage
is pottery in the bird-body kiln

the baby twice-born
blind in its breaking

2

to move backward in time
a slow motion unbraiding

of threads and language
receding toward mother and beyond mother
seed return to cloud, cloud return to sea

tides collapse in gradients of dark
to search blindly in the earth

a downward push toward the question
of water, the numbers fall off the clock

and become a trail of footsteps in the desert
I read all my books backward
until there is only salt in my mouth

I wake up and find the origin
is not where I left it

3

Loyal to the nest, a pair
of storks will fly back to Poland
from Africa every year as they have
to antique nests hundreds of years old

nine feet deep and six wide.
They may or may not deliver
your baby or protect the house
from fire but they will, unlike so much

in this life, return. To ease
abandonment, go back to the mother-
land, place a wagon wheel on your ancestor's
roof or weave a platform of vine.

Leave branches and rags across the grass,
their steel shadows will bear your arrival.

4

braided straw
twigs
bits of wild
cucumber vine

frayed red ribbon
caterpillar silk
intention
auburn hair loosed

from a brush
dried mud
one hundred circlings
round the alder branch

the bright piccolo of morning
a mouth-spun bowl

5

In Oklahoma dawn, the boy
Everett lifted on tiptoe
to collect eggs from the upper shelves
of the chicken house, his palm

reaching beyond sight
for the familiar curvature
still warm in the downy straw
but one morning he grazed

instead a sleeping rattle
snake who lay in the coiled
nest of its body. To think *egg*
and receive *snake*, what newly

emptied matter, what rough field
would steal a father from the wheat?

6

So much like elegy, all
this doing and undoing.
Birches slim to silhouettes,
the cord hollows, a downy

wood-become-soil,
background turns to foreground
and so it goes. Sear and sow.
Shall we call it knowledge—

the deliberate negotiations
the living have with the dead?
An etymology of falling
in a fallen world.

The kindling is a prelude,
the fragments hatch a light.

7

Mound, scrape, pendant, a woman too
fashioned one spring a chair using only what
she found in her yard, a solitary place to sit
or simply proclaim *sitting* among walnut trees.

As she worked lilac branch into catalpa, scrub into pine
a wren built its own cup from her scraps,
lichen, horsebark, strands of silver loosened at dusk.
Both worked in this way, one humming the other's

dumb song into a thin moment of completion
then sat above and below in that speckled wood
neither knowing of the other, the blind way
water bloats the seed into sprout and our bodies work

or do not, the way all action comes from
unknowing and flows back into it as source.

(say we're struck
some low nightgoing song
the body carries since birth
or beyond, maybe *egg* is the first
thought, offspring like a mute call
backward into no river

(See. See again the way darkness
is a net through which light falls.)

what zero gathers forward
what loose chaff binds
the fallen milk of memory
whether we will it or not
we basket we nest a sea
of unspeakable futures)

9

Adrift for a summer in a monastery
I spent evenings with a Ukranian woman
who taught me how to paint eggs.
One technique was to tap a hole at the base,

let yolk, white, drain out.
She felt this was disrespectful
so we traced wax flowers with small knives,
each canvas on the cusp of shattering.

You cannot clasp it for even an instant.
Your concentration must be sweet.
We dipped them in pools of lapis and teal,
confessed darknesses without judgment.

Months later when the inside dried
the egg rattled like a new language.

10

When gifted an ostrich egg
I was told I could stand on it.
There was a dime-shaped hole
at the wide end where

it had been emptied
of its thick gloss. I palmed
the mottled shell
more like blown bone

and sighed into its walls.
An oceanic sound answered
in return and what is a flute
but an accident

of wind singing through
the hollows of the earth?

11

Strange they also fare as weaponry,
rotten eggs stored months in advance
or *blood-eggs*, fertilized without incubus.
Dozens stashed in backpacks

boys sneak out of windows
to mark the plot of outcast or bully,
hurl into flight the maraca shake
of breaking, houses crusted with the hard

shine of yolken glue in dawn's
slatted light. Or one small town's
annual fight as rogue resolution—
is it life they are celebrating or death—

on a three-count of flung-hatching,
the air tossed with a year of grievances.

12

One winter-into-spring, I lived on a farm
with adults who had Down syndrome.
Every day we gathered eggs
from the coop and slagging down

the hillside it was *where are we going?*
and every day I answered *eggs.*
Smooth as china, some were speckled
with blood, double-yolked

or cracked open on hay beds.
I held the cool weight
up to the light
this is an egg, tiny clock

of its own making, the shape
of wonder serious on our faces.

13

Every nest a choice among the vulnerable:
telephone pole, church spire
awning of the New York Stock Exchange.
Who are we to discern function from beauty:

leaf-rot curved inside the bright O
of a McDonald's sign or perched
along the door jamb of the abandoned
concentration camp, starlings

wet among the ash. Consider
the loon who anchors a floating
nest over salt-waves, each egg
its own sea-above-the-sea

tossing while the moon waxes,
to break black into that thrust body.

14

Make of my body a home, I was
an hourglass of salt,
a tarot of bone. Lay me down
under Perseids, let the stars

hold up the night.
I saw for both of us—
tule elk silent among ferns,
sunset lying pink over a field of corn.

Walking through a hall of Buddhas,
the lotus curves shone cold in the half-dark.
Granite. Terra cotta. Bronze.
If I could have made you like that—

I would have held the hammer,
I would have opened the stone.

gloss and grain

The Embryologist

guards a warm room the color of shell.

Master of filament and scale,
her language is revealed

cell by cell

as she holds the first commas
of matter flickering in the ash.

Shepherd y into x

through the zona gate,
love is not math

but a salvage of decibels

in wombglass.
Tend the hearted complex

distilled to source—

so much leans on *perhaps*—
those monkish hours that beg division

more like epilogue.

Evening comes and she drives home past the sea
of yellow grasses

noiseless bells in her ears

urging gloss and grain
blink forward

into the portrait of time.

In the Winter before Everything

I dug a stick into the yard
and watched it disappear and emerge
as the calendar of snow and not-snow
measured us, two huge pairs of eyes
fixed at the window
scavenging for a rind
of sun. We drove into night-
blizzards following the vague trail
of semis toward cheap motels
near the doctor where,
pre-dawn, we'd shiver
the triggered egg toward the target.
In the slant-light of morning
owls were suspended in trees and plastic bags
hooked on toothy branches like defeated
parachutes. We saw every possibility
nesting in a lockbox,
each matchstick of light insinuating
a farmhouse, a family
with their own quiet mercies.
We held each other as pots of soup
simmered on the stove
and did not speak for a long time,
but when we did, we agreed
to believe there were lives
that needed saving before they were born.
No scroll of proof, no
nod from the god-quiet. We did not
know another year later, our son
would sleep inside me where for a brief time
I would be able to give him everything.
And yet.
The stick remained in its earthy plot.
The frost began to resemble a face.

Seen from Above

Steady the freight trains
like daily missives
from other-where—

our stop on the map,
the dislocation of winter's
bandwidth.

Steady now the icicles
freezing in their gravity,
last leaves winnowing

off the tree
and steady the people
with their clocksongs

and filled-up lives
while a few of us are dropping
away like chaff from a scythe.

Emptiness.
Pour the water.
Keep the fire lit.

Things are not as they seem.
To ring the bell
you must give your whole self

over to the bell-rope.
You must lift both feet
off the ground.

Setting the Table for the Deer

Under the ponderosa pine, a family
of deer gathered in late autumn,
chewing on chucked corncobs from August dinners
or our windfall of mealy tree-apples.
Some snowy nights dark with solstice
they'd rush the yard kicking up drifts
under the spun sky
as if beauty had finally sprung a lock
on the reserve midwinter requires.
My father wanted to fell the pine,
its hulking shadow dwarfing the porch,
but was persuaded to let it die
in its own time.
My sisters and I are grown,
our swing-set hung with bird feeders
and the picnic table, migrated
to the woods' edge.
Maybe because the neighborhood has emptied
of children and hammers no longer
pound in the distance,
a new season of deer has returned
and just before my parents dine
at the tidy hour of 5:30,
they carry heaped trays out back, like demigods
lay a spread of alfalfa, oats, clover
along the table's weathered periphery
and the deer emerge in fives and tens,
bend their necks to the splintered planks
where platters of hot dogs and citronella candles
once were, to eat their evening meal,
each with a measured plot of molasses and grain,
the last cinders of dusk falling into place
while inside the house, my father draws
the struck match to the candlewicks,
my mother setting the table for two.

Sea-change

after the waiting years   the leaden

keening oceanside for an answer

from the original dark   you emerge

distinct   one life perpetually not-there

not-to-come

then   suddenly at work with long division

sac of cells we

watched in the flux

out of via negativa

you eddy forth   littlebluefish

littlebigheart

to be here with me now

means we made a study of

insistence   means

I will not forget

the profound absence from which

you began

Barn Owls

Equinox. Apples.
Walnuts dropping from the trees.

A wheel loosens from a cart
and veers down a dirt road.

In the woody rafters,
two barn owls

tilt their ears
to the heartbeats of mice

scurrying the hay bales,
two faces brushed white

with sleep.
A windfall of forms

sharpens against the void.
Fluted sea of cornstalks

back-lit in a ground fog.
The gourds blink silent and human.

Twenty Weeks

We peeked into the fishbowl galaxy today
to view your recent work—

nebula of breath,
thumbprints from the moon.

We've lost touch with our own intricacy,
somewhere in the torque and wick of age

the hardscrabble bones,
but you are a kind of faith

orbiting the sonar,
blood's low note a-swish.

It's blizzarding again
and we are behind glass

silence piling up all around us.
Spin the half-made body

no upside, no down
king of no falling

lassoing the dark.
Tell us what we can't remember.

There in the lit cocoon
we watched each wet yawn and stretch.

Fine boy,
the most important work you'll do,

shape the four chambers
of your heart.

Elegy at Thirty Weeks

—For Everett J. Sweeney

the bagpipes did play for you, *of-the-plains*
did cry out across the march

grasses cold in their histories
wheat father   wind

father-in-the-drum
stories spinning round your chair

a boy, you wrote in January,
impossible

son born into a name
fading out of future

play him piano oh danny boy a Sooner song
banjo on my knee and Cherokee shuffle

what I want you to know: this greenleaf boy
will learn his breath in the hollow

of your flute, will sit with me
in an empty theater listening to a man

rehearse bagpipes all afternoon—
will that be you marching the unlit stage?—

I see you now, oceanside, running
after your own son, clapping into his flight

carved from silence
carved from prairie light

you are in and of the rough matter of our days
we are living your life

Wolf Lake

Seedfluff gathers in white canals along the path
but how to locate the source:
some bramble let-go into all possible

green. April and craving
the fixity of an object.
To hear the bullfrog and see it at once.

The blueprint of spring revealed
itself so briefly at dawn.
For two hours I could see,

outlining the trees,
a presence like slipping
between the margins of loss.

Turtle on the path now.
Thirteen moons painted on its shell.
And the blueprint of the boy

tucked in its sac:
instructions for eyes, nerves, spine.
Waiting for the window

to the next world to open, I say
there is no earthly knowledge like this
but so many minor gladnesses.

Blackbird. Cricket. Clay.
Tulips flouncing open at midnight.
Lightening in the belly,

not long before the last sea gasp.
Instincts we are born with:
suck, cry, sleep,

to stand before a body
of water and want
to throw the palmed stone in.

Tornado Siren

I will remember clutching the ice packs
to my breasts, the way the milk came in,
throttle and burn, so suddenly present
it was a kind of action lunging my body
forward and how the Midwest sky was swollen
with humidity, the cumulonimbus gone
green-black by evening. Four days old,
your body all liquid and howl I gathered
awkwardly in my arms and rocked
past midnight which meant nothing to you,
tornado sirens spinning blue circles
across the city and the ground churned
beneath our dilapidated craftsman.
I will remember how we carried you
down to the rickety cobweb dark where you nursed
next to the hundred-year boiler
as the sky wailed and the bare bulb cut
on and off. To have given everything we had
to get you this side of earth and the wind
funneling up a destruction with no god in it,
how terribly small we became
in a throwaway lawn chair
waiting for a freight train
to snatch the house like a dry husk
or pass us by indifferent. I never rested easy
in your pre-life and here, throbbingly new, the world
continued to bleat *forsake nothing*.
I saw the way anyone would scream
after what they loved in the moment
before the roof fell up or in
as I later watched the faces of Joplin, Missouri
of those who had stashed themselves in salvaged
corners peering out in the wrecked silence
of morning. I will remember
how I understood nothing of what I saw,
the splayed neighborhoods and flattened depots,
love spared or taken,
and how we were raw with beginning, the sobriety
of motherhood anchored me inside
where a white fortress of love and milk
began to shudder into place.

The Nightbird's Apprentice

Douse the lampwick's last light
flood the room with a monsoon
of static, tiny grief-birds

whistling from the attic
(you do not) go down easy
your newly discovered hands

wringing fits of air
there, the first gate cries in return,
its overvining shadows throw a landscape

against the wall
clench and release, your body
one muscle held against the night.

The second gate is a plane of sound
cicadas scissor the grass
rainwater drips into bottles and you

buck the dark, darkling
yodel your oval wind, fall
upward as we open the third gate

suspended in catalpa trees, please
follow we promise no death
this daily lying down a human thing.

We will row you, lotus you
tra-la and river you
while the one-handed clock

tocks half-truths.
Come, grow vague with us,
fidget the sky.

Nest: Revisited

On the same corner of Oak
two years to the day
the twiggy bowl reappeared at my feet

downturned, eggless,
struck from the horizontal
winds of May

perhaps from the same unsteady branch
or spun from the same
effort of return,

this time with strips of corrugated
plastic woven into its thicket
shaped against a potter's mud.

I carried it home in my right hand,
guided the stroller with my left,
buoyant and exhausted

with love, the tease of symbols
having lost its charge,
loss no longer the lens

through which I attribute magic
and that gulleywash—hope—
though every hunter's moon

and crushed blue egg ached
when my hands were huge
in their emptiness, it was my hunger

for such signs that kept me
lashed to the present.
Divination of happenstance,

map with a collage
of trinkets for a key.
Though none of it

mattered, this hollow
trust I knelt each day
before the gods.

Orbit Song

For everything beaten and beating

the bright scars of uranium

glowing in a private dark

every dark bowl the poplars

gather on thin branches

breaking and broken each

mechanical heart stitched

in its moorings the body

radiating from the courageous

love of its gears

For everything moored and unmoored

space operas careening

through black holes loosed and singing

glass notes along a mile's curve

and each silence arrow-shot

into moments *before* and *after*

with their own kind of white bass,

all fragments and kindnesses

born of blue ice, the blue scrim

of beyond that locates the tiny

helix on its stem

For every aberration, every

rift and swell when blueprint

slid away and the cell mass

swerved from its knowing

and knowing no fathom forward

began so many futures

the breath the split light

every dry mouth eaten and eating

Acknowledgments

I am grateful to the editors of the following journals, in which these poems appeared, sometimes in an earlier form:

American Poetry Review: "Little Spells," "Twenty Weeks"

Aperçus Quarterly: "Barn Owls," "The Nightbird's Apprentice," "Study of Family with Buckets," and "Still Life with Egg #2, 3, 5, 6, 7, 8, 10, 11, 12, 13"

Black Tongue Review: "Still Life with Egg #14" as "The Rehearsal," "Tendril-minded"

Cavewall: "Seen From Above," parts 1 and 3 of "Aubade for the Thirteenth Hour," "Nest: Revisited"

Connotation Press: An Online Artifact: "Sea-change"

Crab Orchard Review: "Tornado Siren"

Hayden's Ferry Review: "White October," "The Dance Student"

Hunger Mountain: "Happy People"

Jet Fuel Review: "The Blueberry Pickers" as "Blueberries in Michigan," "Field Accomplice"

Meridian: "Beyond a Longing Lying Bluely," "Blindness Training Center," "The Embryologist"

Mid-American Review: "Winter, Parenthetical" as "Parenthetical at 35"

New American Writing: "Hans-my-Hedgehog," "Sleeping Beauty," "Tatterhood"

Passages North: "The Returning"

Pebble Lake Review: "The Stone Fitter"

Ping-Pong: "Across Useless Bay," "Still Life with Egg #10" as "Equinox"

Puerto del Sol: "Gingerbread Man," "Rapunzel," "Thumbelina"

Quay: part 2 of "Aubade for the Thirteenth Hour" as "Mating Season"

Southern Humanities Review: "In the Winter before Everything," "Vespertine"

Spillway: "Still Life with Egg #6" as "Variation on Source"

Subtropics: "Sleep Theory," "Still Life with Egg # 1 and 4"

Sweet: "Call and Response," "Wolf Lake," "Setting the Table for the Deer," "Janice Pockett," "On Not Being an Axeman"

"Study of Family with Buckets," "Still Life with Egg #14" (as "Inviting the Child"), "Barn Owls," and "The Nightbird's Apprentice" were awarded Dorothy Sargent Rosenberg prizes.

"Abandoning the Hives" was printed as a limited edition broadside by Oneiros Press.

"Seen from Above" was featured on *Verse Daily*.

"Call and Response," "Wolf Lake," "Setting the Table for the Deer" were included in the anthology, *All of Us: Sweet: The First Five Years*.

Deepest thanks to my friends on the path who read and commented on poems in this collection: Traci Brimhall, Katherine Case, Patricia Caspers, Lauren Henley, Gary McDowell, Annie Stenzel, Rachel Swearingen, Rhett Iseman Trull, and especially Chad Sweeney who bears loving witness to the making of these poems and all the life breathing beneath them.

Notes

Opening text is from Margaret Atwood's *The Handmaid's Tale*.

"Happy People" is for my father, Richard Kochanek, after his silkscreen of the same title.

"On Not Being an Axeman" is indebted to the essay, "On Tools" by Lia Purpura.

Short Anthology of Fairytales:

> There are countless folk and fairy tales depicting women who desired children but struggled or were unable to bear them. These characters are repeatedly portrayed in the negative as silent, unfit, shriveled, jealous, flawed, pitiable, incomplete, marginal, desperate, relying on magic, and bargaining with the devil.

> *Hans-my-Hedgehog* involves a couple who was unable to have a child until the woman says, "I wouldn't care if he were ugly as a hedgehog!"—whereupon she has a baby who looks like a hedgehog.

> *The Iroko Tree or Iroko Man / Oluronbi* is a Yoruba legend that highlights the common theme of a barren woman seeking magic realms to conceive and then being asked to return the child to the provider, in this case the dangerous Iroko-tree man.

> Many versions of *Sleeping Beauty* begin with a king and queen who long for a child and cannot conceive. A daughter is finally born after a long and mournful period of infertility. To celebrate her christening, her godmothers invite seven fairies to bestow a gift to the baby girl. A very old fairy, believed to be dead and thus uninvited, comes to the celebration, rumored to be bringing an unlucky gift. She announces the princess will have her hand pierced with a spindle and die of the wound. One of the fairies steps forward, and though she cannot undo this curse entirely, says that the daughter will not die, but rather fall into a hundred-year sleep, the duration of sleep representative of infertility itself, the inactive waiting, a period of life-on-hold.

> *Snow White*: After King Midas's wife drank a vile potion that rendered her infertile, the couple adopted Prince Charming, but the king could not get over the "curse" of infertility and claimed his adopted son had made his suffering worse and

must, therefore, be made to share his pain. When Midas meets Charming's true love, Snow White, he puts the same curse in her goblet to render her infertile.

Tatterhood is a Norwegian fairy tale in which a beggar woman tells a queen she will be able to have children if she eats one of two flowers, warning her to only eat the pretty one. The queen eats both the pretty and ugly flower and bears two daughters of opposite personalities.

The story of *Thumbelina* begins with a childless woman wishing to bear a child. After visiting a fairy who gives her a magical barleycorn, she plants the flower and kisses the leaves. A tulip opens, and a tiny daughter emerges from the stamens. This portion of the story portrays the tender wish and intimacy between mother and daughter, and then the mother all but disappears from the story with no further mention, infertility seeming to be a disposable and handy plot construction.

Janice Pockett disappeared at the age of 7 in Tolland, Connecticut, July 1973. Charges have never been filed against anyone regarding her disappearance, and her case remains unsolved. I was born in 1973 and grew up in Tolland from birth to college.

"Blindness Training Center": I lived about a mile from the *Michigan Commission for the Blind Training Center* in Kalamazoo which provides blindness training to the newly-blind and to those whose vision is deteriorating.

Useless Bay is a remote bay on South Whidbey Island, Washington; the name given by early seafaring explorers as the tidal mudflats make the bay useless to boats for anchoring purposes. At low tide, one can walk over a quarter mile across the mudflats and into the sea.

"Study of Family with Buckets" is for the O'Neill family at Eastham, Cape Cod.

"The Blueberry Pickers": In 2009, an ABC news investigation, entitled "The Blueberry Children," exposed child labor practices at the Adkin Blue Ribbon Packing Company in South Haven, Michigan where child workers as young as five were found. Seven other blueberry farms were also implicated.

"Elegy at Thirty Weeks" is in memory of Everett John Sweeney, 3/21/1945 -3/7/2010.

Wolf Lake is located in Western Michigan.

"Tornado Siren" mentions the town of Joplin, Missouri which was devastated by an EF-5 tornado on May 22, 2011. This tornado was the deadliest since modern record keeping began in 1950.

"Orbit Song" draws inspiration from Sandra Alcosser's line, "For everything eating and eaten."

photo by Kimberley Clay

Little Spells is Jennifer K. Sweeney's third book of poetry. Her
second book, *How to Live on Bread and Music* (Perugia Press Prize, 2009),
won the James Laughlin Award from the Academy of American Poets and
was nominated for the Poets' Prize. Her first collection, *Salt Memory,* won
the Main Street Rag Poetry Award in 2006. Sweeney's poems have appeared
in *The Pushcart Prize Anthology*, *Poetry Daily*, *American Poetry Review*,
New American Writing, *Pleiades*, *Verse Daily*, and the *Academy of
American Poets "Poem-a-Day"* series. After earning her MFA from Vermont
College, she has served as visiting writer at Kalamazoo College and at
multiple writing festivals and retreats. She teaches workshops and offers
manuscript consultation in California where she lives with her husband, poet
Chad Sweeney, and their sons, Liam and Forest.